T0193253

KITCHEN PROJECT MANAGEMENT

KITCHEN PROJECT MANAGEMENT

THE ART AND SCIENCE OF AN ORGANIZED KITCHEN

DEJI BADIRU AND
ISWAT BADIRU

KITCHEN PROJECT MANAGEMENT
THE ART AND SCIENCE OF AN ORGANIZED KITCHEN

iUniverse books may be ordered through booksellers or by contacting:

iUniverse
1663 Liberty Drive
Bloomington, IN 47403
www.iuniverse.com
1-800-Authors (1-800-288-4677)

ISBN: 978-1-5320-8856-8 (sc)
ISBN: 978-1-5320-8857-5 (e)

Print information available on the last page.

iUniverse rev. date: 11/29/2019

Adedeji Badiru writes as the primary author for ABICS Publications (www.abicspublications.com), a division of AB International Consulting Services, dedicated to publishing books for home, work, and leisure.

ABICS Publications

A Division of
AB International Consulting Services (ABICS)

www.ABICSPublications.com

Books for home, work, and leisure

(ABICSURUS reader, mascot of ABICS Publications,
with seductive reading eyes graphics)

Books in the ABICS Publications book series, published by iUniverse, Inc., on recreational, educational, motivational, and personal development books, include the titles below:

Kitchen Project Management: The Art and Science of an Organized Kitchen

Wives of the Same School: Tributes and Straight Talk

The Rooster and The Hen: The Story of Love at Last Look

Kitchen Physics: Dynamic Nigerian Recipes

The Story of Saint Finbarr's College: Contributions to Education and Sports Development in Nigeria

Physics of Soccer II: Science and Strategies for a Better Game

Kitchen Dynamics: The rice way

Consumer Economics: The value of dollars and sense for money management

Youth Soccer Training Slides: A Math and Science Approach

My Little Blue Book of Project Management

8 by 3 Paradigm for Time Management

Badiru's Equation of Student Success: Intelligence, Common Sense, and Self-discipline

Isi Cookbook: Collection of Easy Nigerian Recipes

Blessings of a Father: Education contributions of Father Slattery at Saint Finbarr's College

Physics in the Nigerian Kitchen: The Science, the Art, and the Recipes

The Physics of Soccer: Using Math and Science to Improve Your Game

Getting things done through project management

CONTENTS

DEDICATION

This book is dedicated to all those who struggle with getting their kitchen chores done on time, on quality, and within budget.

ACKNOWLEDGMENTS

We acknowledge the contributions of our family, friends, and colleagues, who create opportunities to demonstrate our commitment to kitchen excellence. Food, family, fun, fellowship, and faith represent the underpinning of what we do in our kitchen and the people around us provide the environment and motivation for practicing what we preach about project management in the kitchen.

CHAPTER ONE

Introduction

The premise of this book is to advocate the application of project management in the kitchen, just as it is applied in business and industry applications. Although the kitchen environment is devoid of the complexity encountered in other projects, such as construction, the same level of dedication to the cause is required in the kitchen. Of all the elements of project management, planning is of the most critical need in the kitchen. Thus, the application of rigorous project management in the kitchen is a legitimate approach to making the kitchen less stressful.

Everything is a project. A project is everything to the success and welfare of human kind. Nowhere is this more aptly true than in a culinary kitchen. The basis of human existence is food as a source of nourishment. The primary product of any kitchen is food. Whether the kitchen is formal or informal, commercial or charitable, public or private, corporate or personal, the same desired end product is food. It does make sense that we dedicate ourselves to how to prepare food in any kitchen as a project execution within time, quality, and budget constraints.

This book is about the application of project management tools and techniques to kitchen activities. Project management is one of the hottest topics in the business world because it is through project management that organizational goals and objectives are pursued and accomplished. The same rigorous tools and techniques of project management used in the corporate world can and should be applied in the kitchen.

Kitchen project management is about getting more done in the kitchen in a limited amount of time, in an organized and less stressful way. There is both science and art interplaying in the kitchen. Project management can help enmesh both for the benefit of a successful kitchen output.

The kitchen is central to most homes. As such, we offer the following kitchen project invocation:

"Give us life and love, fellowship and faith, and
free pursuit of flavor in our kitchen."

Special holidays and events, such as Thanksgiving, Christmas, July 4th, Memorial Day, and Mothers' Day, offer unique crowd-hosting opportunities to practice kitchen project management. Happy hosting!

Who are the authors?

As of September 2019, Deji and Iswat have been married for 44 years. They have shared their mutual love of successful kitchen projects over all those years. Although they are not professional kitchen connoisseurs, their commitment to excellence in the kitchen comes through in all their engagements. Over the years, they have hosted a diversity of guests, who always marvel at the effortless rendition of their kitchen-management expertise. Deji is professionally an engineer and fervently practices the reputation of engineers as problem solvers. He prides himself in an unusual entry in his curriculum vitae that points to his avocation of kitchen science experiments. He enjoys multi-faceted cooking, dancing, painting, and writing He takes an artistic view of kitchen pursuits. In one of their previous cooking-oriented books, Deji wrote odes and poems, two of which are echoed below:

Deji's Ode to Rice

Rice, in my hot water, you rise magically.
You are the rice of my soul.
You are the rise of my day.
You are the apple of my eye.
When I see you, I salivate.
I live for you, you grow for me.
What a nice partnership that is!
You make me rise every morning;
You are the springboard of my day;
Each day, I rise to relish my rice;
The anchor of my recipe;
The root of my existence;
Without you, I am nothing but jelly;
I dream of you when I miss you on my plate;
Yes, you are my pot's soul mate;
You are the very nice rice of my soul.
May you always rest in perfect harmony with my plate!

Deji's Ode to the Arts of Cooking, Dancing, Painting, and Writing

Behold;
The dance of meat molecules in my pot;
The dance of my pen on paper;
The dance of my paintbrush on canvas;
Oh;
The tangle, twist, and tango of my feet on the dance floor;
It's all Arts to me.

Ingredients are to the recipe what paint hues are to the portrait;
Steps are to the dance what pen strokes are to the script;
And;
Of course, cooking, dancing, painting, and writing are, to me, the very existence.
Of what is life without The Arts?

Iswat is a homemaker, whose college degrees are in interior design and management information systems. She has offered countless help sessions in cooking events and specializes in single-handed large-scale cooking for various audiences, large or small. She dabbles in informal catering of social events. Deji and Iswat enjoy world travels, where they can sample diverse ethnic foods, particularly tasty and indigenous street foods that exhibit a lot of flavor punch and tempting spectacles to the eyes.

CHAPTER TWO

What is Project Management?

Project management is the process of managing,
allocating, and timing resources to achieve a
given objective in an expeditious manner.

Based on the concise nature and application orientation of this book, only an abridged coverage of project management is presented here. Interested readers are referred to the comprehensive project management bibliography at the end of this chapter. The bibliography demonstrates the wide applications of project management in various and diverse areas.

Project management has global applications in all types of pursuits. It is a common language of getting things done, ranging from primitive villages to much advanced communities. Project management is applicable to all human endeavors, including engineering firms, legal enterprises, production facilities, political organizations, transportation systems, home care facilities, job search, shopping, construction, manufacturing, education, neighborhood watch, supply chain, health care, home remodeling, public service, customer service, sales, and, yes, kitchen activities.

Whatever the project is, it can be done through project management. Project management skills are needed and highly valued in every organization.

What is a Project?

- A project is a plan or program performed by the people with assigned resources to achieve an objective within a finite duration.
- A project is a temporary endeavor undertaken to create a unique product, service, or result. "Temporary" means that every project has a definite beginning and a definite end.
- Projects have specified objectives to be completed within certain specifications and funding limits.
- Projects are often critical components of the performing organization's business strategy.

What is a project objective?

- A description of the project's expected outcome
- Direct output of the project
- Timed expectation, short-term or long-term
- Bounded parameters of the project within a defined scope

The objectives of a project may be stated in terms of time (schedule), performance (quality), or cost (budget). The output of a project, such as a kitchen project, may be defined in terms of the following categories:

- A physical end product (e.g., a culinary dish)

- A service (e.g., community meal service)
- A result (e.g., a specific flavor)

Time is often the most critical aspect of managing any project. Time must be managed concurrently with all other important aspects of any project, particularly in a kitchen setting. Project management covers the basic stages listed below:

1. Project concept and initiation
2. Project planning
3. Project execution
4. Project tracking
5. Project control
6. Project closure

The stages are often shortened or expanded based on the needs of the specific project. They can also overlap based on the prevailing project scenarios. For example, tracking and control often occur concurrently with project execution. Embedded within execution is the function of activity scheduling. If shortened, the list of stages may include only planning, organizing, scheduling, and control. In this case, closure is seen as a control action. If expanded, the list may include additional explicit stages such as conceptualization, scoping, resource allocation, and reporting.

Project Initiation

In the first stage of the project lifecycle, the scope of the project is defined along with the approach to be taken to deliver the desired results. The project manager and project team are appointed based on skills, experience, and relevance. The process of organizing the project is often carried out as a bridge or overlap between initiation and planning. The most common tools used in the initiation stage are Project Charter, Business Plan, Project Framework, Overview, Process

Mapping, Business Case Justification, and Milestone Reviews. Project initiation normally takes place after problem identification and project definition.

Project Planning

The second stage of the project lifecycle includes a detailed identification and assignment of tasks making up the project. It should also include a risk analysis and a definition of criteria for the successful completion of each deliverable. During planning, the management process is defined, stakeholders are identified, reporting frequency is established, and communication channels are agreed upon. The most common tools used in the planning stage are Brainstorming, Business Plan, Process Mapping, and Milestones Reviews. In this case, planning and time management will be the core aspects of project management in the kitchen.

Execution and Control

The most important issue in the execution and control stages of the project lifecycle involves ensuring that tasks are executed expeditiously in accordance with the project plan, which is always subject to re-planning. Tracking is an implicit component and prerequisite for project control. For projects that are organized for producing physical products, a design resulting in a specific set of product requirements is created. The integrity of the product is assured through prototypes, validation, verification, and testing. As the execution phase progresses, groups across the organization become progressively involved in the realization of the project objectives. The most common tools or methodologies used in the execution stage include Risk Analysis, Balance Scorecards, Business Plan Review, and Milestone Assessment.

Project Closure

In the closure stage, the project is phased-out or formally terminated. The closure process is often gradual as the project is weaned of resources and personnel are reallocated to other organizational needs. Acceptance of deliverables is an important part of project closure. The closure phase is characterized by a written formal project review report containing the following components: a formal acceptance of the final product, Weighted Critical Measurements (matching the initial requirements with the final product delivered), rewarding the team, a list of lessons learned, releasing project resources, and a formal project closure notification to management and other stakeholders. A common tool for project closure is Project Closure Report.

Of course, not all elements in the above outline will be applicable to a kitchen project in a personal home. The point here is to be cognizant of the full scope of project management steps, such that only the applicable steps are applied to a kitchen endeavor. This is particularly important since more kitchen projects will be limited to a few people (even one person), compared to the multitude of people involved in corporate projects. The fewer the number of people involved in a project, the less complicated the project. Thus, a project in the kitchen is more manageable and controllable, from the perspective of human interfaces. Project management in the kitchen then simplifies to the commitment of the individual person (cook or chef) to apply the steps of project management unilaterally.

Management By Project

Project management continues to grow as an effective means of managing functions in any organization. Project management should be an enterprise-wide and systems-based endeavor. Enterprise-wide project management is the application of project management techniques and practices across the full scope of the enterprise. This concept is also referred to as management by project (MBP). MBP is a contemporary concept that employs project management techniques in various functions within an organization. MBP recommends pursuing endeavors as project-oriented activities. It is an effective way to conduct any business activity. It represents a disciplined approach that defines any work assignment as a project. Under MBP, every undertaking is viewed as a project that must be managed just like a traditional project. The characteristics required of each project so defined are summarized below:

1. An identified scope and a goal
2. A desired completion time
3. Availability of resources
4. A defined performance measure
5. A measurement scale for review of work

An MBP approach to operations helps in identifying unique entities within functional requirements. This identification helps determine where functions overlap and how they are interrelated, thus paving the way for better planning, scheduling, and control. Enterprise-wide project management facilitates a unified view of organizational goals and provides a way for project teams to use information generated by other departments to carry out their functions.

The need to develop effective management tools increases with the increasing complexity of new technologies and processes. The life cycle of a new product to be introduced into a competitive market is a good example of a complex process that must be managed with integrative project management approaches. The product will encounter management functions as it goes from one stage to the next. Project management will be needed throughout the design and production stages of the product. Project management will be needed in developing marketing, transportation, and delivery strategies for the product. When the product finally gets to the customer, project management will be needed to integrate its use with those of other products within the customer's organization.

Laws for Project Management

The need for a project management approach is established by the fact that a project will always tend to increase in size even if its scope is narrowing. There are several guiding principles for project management. These are presented here as common laws of project management. They serve as philosophical and practical guidelines. Although they were not developed specifically for project management, they are aptly applicable since every undertaking is seen as a project. Thus, they are presented here as the laws for project management.

- **Murphy's Law**
"Whatever can go wrong will."
Translation:- Project planning must make allowance for contingencies. This is one of the most commonly cited laws of project management.

- **Parkinson's Law**
"Work expands to fill the available time."
Translation:- Idle time in project schedule creates opportunity for ineffective utilization of time.

- **Peter's Principle**
"People rise to the level of their incompetence."
Translation:- Get the right person into the right job.

- **Badiru's Theory**
"Grass is always greener where you most need it to be dead."
Translation:- Problems fester naturally if left alone. Control must be exercised in order to preempt problems. Don't concede to others what you can control yourself.

An integrated systems project management approach can help diminish the adverse impacts of these laws through good project planning, organizing, scheduling, and control.

There is a lot going on in the kitchen. It is only on a close examination, from a project management perspective, that all the intricacies can be seen. Any misstep in any of the critical components of a kitchen can lead to a disastrous kitchen output. The project management wheel of function presented in (Figure 2.1 shows the various elements and stages of executing a project. As simple as the operational setting of a kitchen might appear to be, there is still a lot of complexity embedded within the functions. All of the elements shown in the figure must be coordinated and controlled tightly to ensure a successful output of the kitchen. Ensuring a successful kitchen output is the premise of this book. Apply project management, and you will see good kitchen results.

Figure 2.1. Project Management Wheel Function in the Kitchen

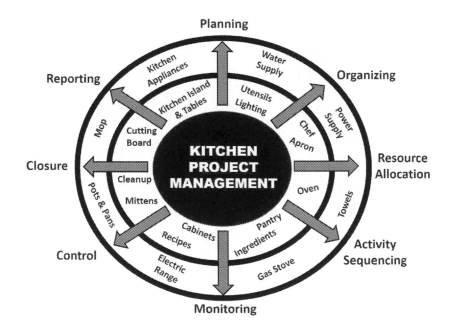

Recommended Project Management Bibliography

Badiru, A. B. (2019), **Project Management: Systems, Principles, and Applications**, Second Edition, Taylor & Francis CRC Press, Boca Raton, FL.

Badiru, A. B., S. Abi Badiru, and I. Ade Badiru, (2019), **Mechanics of Project Management: Nuts and Bolts of Project Execution,** Taylor & Francis/CRC Press, Boca Raton, FL.

Badiru, A. B., Christina F. Rusnock, and Vhance V. Valencia (2016), **Project Management for Research: A Guide for Graduate Students**, Taylor & Francis CRC Press, Boca Raton, FL.

Badiru, A. B. and S. O. Osisanya (2013), **Project Management for the Oil & Gas Industry**, Taylor & Francis CRC Press, Boca Raton, FL

Badiru, A. B. (2009), **STEP Project Management: Guide for Science, Technology, and Engineering Projects**, Taylor & Francis CRC Press, Boca Raton, FL.

Badiru, A. B. (2008), **Triple C Model of Project Management: Communication, Cooperation, and Coordination**, Taylor & Francis CRC Press, Boca Raton, FL.

Badiru, A. B.; Abi Badiru; Ade Badiru (2008), **Industrial Project Management: Concepts, Tools, and Techniques**, Taylor & Francis CRC Press, Boca Raton, FL.

Badiru, A. B. (1996), **Project Management in Manufacturing and High Technology Operations**, 2nd edition, John Wiley & Sons, New York.

Badiru, A. B. (1996), **Project Management for Research: A Guide for Engineering and Science**, Chapman & Hall, London, UK.

Badiru, A. B. and P. S. Pulat (1995), **Comprehensive Project Management: Integrating Optimization Models, Management Principles, and Computers**, Prentice-Hall, Englewood Cliffs, NJ.

Badiru, A. B. (1993), **Managing Industrial Development Projects: A Project Management Approach**, Van Nostrand/John Wiley, New York.

CHAPTER THREE

First Principle for Project Management

The first principle for getting things done promptly can be summarized as:

"To get more done, try and do less."

There are little nagging things that consume time every day. They are usually of little or no value. Eliminate them and you will have more discretionary time to yourself. Saving time through project management gives you time to do other things that you really want to do.

If Albert Einstein had attempted to do several things in the years that he was fiddling with his theory of relativity, he probably would not have gotten it done when he did. Leonardo da Vinci (of the Mona Lisa fame) was reputed to not have been a good project manager because he died with several unfinished projects in various stages of incompletion. What would have happened if he had focused on a few projects that were actually finished?

In order to get more done, you need to be more selective with social impositions. Such impositions create more things to do and less time to do the most crucial tasks. You don't have to visit Joe and Jane every time they issue an invitation for a gathering. You don't really have to attend every social function for which you have an invitation, no matter how sumptuous the Hors D'oeuvres might be. Identify what not to do at all. Identify what to do and in what order. Set goals and hold firm to the goals. Flip-flopping between setting goals and dismantling them with inaction does not leave room for actually getting things done.

The first principle is directly applicable in kitchen project management. If you don't have to cook, don't cook. If you have to cook, then do it well coordinated and start early.

Prepare sides and accompaniments in advance or in parallel to compress the overall schedule of the kitchen project.

Haste makes waste just as rush makes crash. Getting more things done requires focusing on fewer things to do. Don't spend time and effort on an activity that has little or no potential for providing value or generating a benefit. This implies that we must "separate the wheat from the chaff" in the kitchen (no pun intended) when deciding on what needs to be done. We must be able to distinguish value-adding activities from wasteful activities. That means, we must operate "lean" and cut out non-value-adding activities in kitchen endeavors. Pareto distribution (also known as A-B-C classification) presents the fact that only about 20% of what we do is actually value-adding. As much as 80% of our activities could be going into less-value-adding engagements.

Studies have shown that trying to do too much often leads to getting less done. Tackling too much makes the "doer" more error prone, thereby leading to rework and subsequent waste of corrective time. If the A-B-C categorization is embraced, we could have the following segmentation of activities:

A Category: Top 10 percent in order of value (very essential)

B Category: Middle 80 percent in order of value (minimally essential).

C Category: Bottom 10 percent in order of value (non-essential).

The C Category is often a "lost cause" and can be eliminated without much adverse consequence. By eliminating this, you will have more time to focus on the essential items. You will, consequently, be getting more done by focusing on fewer essential items.

Simplification helps to get more things done

Too often in life, we allow inconsequential lifestyles activities to rob us of time to get *really* valuable things done. You cannot hem-and-haw all day and then complain that you don't have enough time to get things done. Dilly-dally and shilly-shally ways of project execution rob us of opportunities to get the right things done promptly and satisfactorily.

CHAPTER FOUR

Project Planning

In a kitchen, planning is everything. A plan is the map of the wise. The key to a successful project is good planning. Project planning provides the basis for the initiation, implementation, and termination of a project, setting guidelines for specific project objectives, project structure, tasks, milestones, personnel, cost, equipment, performance, and problem resolutions. The question of whether or not the project is needed at all should be addressed in the planning phase of new projects, as well as an analysis of what is needed and what is available. The availability of technical expertise within the organization and outside the organization should be reviewed. If subcontracting is needed, the nature of the contracts should undergo a thorough analysis. The "make", "buy", "lease", "sub-contract," or "do-nothing" alternatives should be compared as a part of the project planning process. In the initial stage of project planning, both the internal and external factors that influence the project should be determined and given priority weights. Examples of internal influences on project plans include:

- Infrastructure
- Project scope
- Labor relations
- Project location
- Project leadership
- Organizational goal
- Management approach
- Technical manpower supply
- Resource and capital availability.

In addition to internal factors, project plans can be influenced by external factors. An external factor may be the sole instigator of a project, or it may manifest itself in combination with other external and internal factors. Such external factors include the following:

- Public needs
- Market needs
- National goals
- Industry stability
- State of technology
- Industrial competition
- Government regulations.

Strategic planning decisions may be divided into three strategy levels: supra-level planning, macro-level planning, and micro-level planning:

Supra-level Planning: Planning at this level deals with the big picture of how the project fits the overall and long-range organizational goals. Questions faced at this level concern potential contributions of the project to the welfare of the organization, the effect on the depletion of company resources, required interfaces with other projects within and outside the organization, risk exposure, management support for the project, concurrent projects, company culture, market share, shareholder expectations, and financial stability.

Macro-level Planning: Planning decisions at this level address the overall planning within the project boundary. The scope of the project and its operational interfaces should be addressed at this level. Questions faced at the macro level include goal definition, project scope, the availability of qualified personnel and resources, project policies, communication interfaces, budget requirements, goal interactions, deadlines, and conflict-resolution strategies.

Micro-level Planning: This deals with detailed operational plans at the task levels of the project. Definite and explicit tactics for accomplishing specific project objectives are developed at the micro level. The concept of MBO (management by objective) may be particularly effective at this level. MBO permits each project member to plan his or her own work at the micro level. Factors to be considered at the micro level of project decisions include scheduled time, training requirements, tools required, task procedures, reporting requirements, and quality requirements.

Large-scale project planning may need to include a statement about the feasibility of subcontracting part of the project work. Subcontracting or outsourcing may be necessary for various reasons, including lower cost, higher efficiency, or logistical convenience.

Resolving Project Conflicts

Project conflicts should be resolved promptly and amicably. The Triple C, discussed later in Chapter 7), is effective in resolving project conflicts because it is based on clear communication and mutual cooperation. Directional conflicts can mislead participants and stakeholders of a project. Everyone involved must see the project from the same point of view.

When implemented as an integrated process, the Triple C model can help avoid conflicts in a project. When conflicts do develop, it can help in resolving the conflicts. Several types of conflicts can develop in the project environment. Some of these conflicts are listed and discussed below:

Scheduling conflicts: Scheduling conflicts can develop because of improper timing or sequencing of project tasks. This is particularly common in large multiple projects. Procrastination can lead to having too much to do at once, thereby creating a clash of project functions and discord between project team members. Inaccurate estimates of time requirements may lead to unfeasible activity schedules. Project coordination can help avoid schedule conflicts.

Cost conflicts: Project cost may not be generally acceptable to the clients of a project. This will lead to project conflict. Even if the initial cost of the project is acceptable, a lack of cost control during project implementation can lead to conflicts. Poor budget allocation approaches and the lack of financial feasibility study will cause cost conflicts later on in a project. Communication and coordination can help prevent most of the adverse effects of cost conflicts.

Performance conflicts: If clear performance requirements are not established, performance conflicts will develop. A lack of clearly defined performance standards can lead each person to evaluate his or her own performance based on personal value judgments. In order to uniformly evaluate quality of work and monitor project progress, performance standards should be established by using the Triple C approach.

Management conflicts: There must be a two-way alliance between management and the project team. The views of management should be understood by the team. The views of the team should be appreciated by management. If this does not happen, management conflicts will develop. A lack of a two-way interaction can lead to strikes and industrial actions which can be detrimental to project objectives. The Triple C approach can help create a cordial dialogue environment between management and the project team.

Technical conflicts: If the technical basis of a project is not sound, technical conflicts will develop. Manufacturing and automation projects are particularly prone to technical conflicts because of their significant dependence on technology. Lack of a comprehensive technical feasibility study will lead to technical conflicts. Performance requirements and systems specifications can be integrated through the Triple C approach to avoid technical conflicts.

Priority conflicts: Priority conflicts can develop if project objectives are not defined properly and applied uniformly across a project. Lack of direction in project definition can lead each project member to define individual goals that may be in conflict with the intended goal of a project. Lack of consistency of project mission is another potential source of priority conflicts. Over-assignment of responsibilities with no guidelines for relative significance levels can also lead to priority conflicts. Communication can help defuse priority conflicts.

Resource Conflicts: Resource allocation problems are a major source of conflicts in project management. Competition for resources, including personnel, tools, hardware, software, and so on, can lead to disruptive clashes among project members. The Triple C approach can help secure resource cooperation.

Power Conflicts: Project politics can lead to power plays as one individual seeks to widen his or her scope of power. This can, obviously, adversely affect the progress of a project. Project authority and project power should be clearly differentiated: Project authority is the control that a person has by virtue of his or her functional post, while project power relates to the clout and influence which a person can exercise due to connections within the administrative structure. People with popular personalities can often wield a lot of project power in spite of low or nonexistent project authority. The Triple C model can facilitate a positive marriage of project authority and power to the benefit of project goals. This will help define clear leadership for a project.

Personality conflicts: Personality conflicts are a common problem in projects involving a large group of people. The larger a project, the larger the size of the management team needed to keep things running. Unfortunately, the larger management team also creates an opportunity for personality conflicts. Communication and cooperation can help defuse personality conflicts. Some guidelines for resolving project conflicts are presented below:

- Approach the source of conflict.
- Gather all the relevant facts.
- Notify those involved in writing.
- Solicit mediation.
- Report to the appropriate authorities.

CHAPTER FIVE

Activity Sequencing

It is important to sequence activities to determine the most effective order to execute them. This is referred to as activity sequencing, which is the key part of project scheduling. Even simple tasks at home such as cooking, doing laundry, house cleaning, and dressing up do require proper sequencing. The usual stress of multi-tasking to accomplish these chores can be mitigate by smooth sequencing.

Activity sequencing presents the interactions between activities and their precedence relationships. In order to develop an effective project schedule, the following questions should be addressed:

Which activities must come first?
Which activities must follow which ones?
Can some activities be run in series or parallel?
Can some activities be eliminated?
What type and level of dependency exists among activities?

Activity sequencing requires the following items:

1. **Project Scope Statement** – The Project Scope statement describes the characteristics of the project and boundaries of performance. The project scope statement complements the project charter.

2. **Activity List** – The Activity List shows the list of activities making up the project. Activity sequencing is the structural ordering of the activities in the list. Activity list is a breakdown of the project deliverables into their component activities and provide crucial inputs for constructing the Work Breakdown Structure (WBS).

3. **Activity attributes** – Activity attributes specify the individual characteristics of activities. The attributes are important for scheduling, sorting, and arranging the contents of the project. Descriptions of activities often include activity codes, related activities, physical locations, responsible persons, assumptions, and constraints.

4. **Milestones** – Milestones indicate points of significant accomplishments in the project. They indicate progress toward the eventual goal of the project.

The common tools and techniques for activity sequencing are described below:

- **Precedence Diagramming Method (PDM)** - PDM is the most widely used network diagramming method for activity sequencing. It shows activity relationships as start-to-start, start-to-finish, finish-to-start, and finish-to-finish. Each activity is represented by a rectangular block, or node, and linked by arrows to show activity-to-activity dependencies.

- **Arrow Diagramming Method (ADM)** - ADM is a network diagramming method in which activities are shown as arrows. It is sometimes called Activity-On-Arrows. The application of

ADM is limited to finish-to-start relationships among activities. The sequence in which activities should be performed is shown by joining activity arrows at nodes. If desired, dummy activities (dummy nodes) are included to indicate project starting point and overall ending point.

- **Dependency determination** - Determining the types of dependencies (i.e., precedence relationship) is critical to the development of a project network diagram. The three types of dependencies used to define the sequence among the activities are:

  o Mandatory (e.g., technical),
  o Discretionary (e.g., procedural preferences), and
  o External (e.g., imposed requirements).

- **Applying leads and lags** - Using leads and lags allows the logical relationships between activities to be accurately described. A lead allows for bringing forward the next activity or letting it overlap the preceding activity by a given amount of time. A lag allows for delaying the next activity by a given amount of time or project space.

Sequencing can be performed by using project management software, manual techniques, or a combination of both. The end result of activity sequencing is the network diagram that provides a graphical representation of project activities, milestones, objectives, goals, and the order in which they need to be accomplished. It is helpful to widely disseminate the network diagram so everyone can see and understand exactly where each person fits in the overall project scheme.

Activity sequencing results in outputs which assist in scheduling project activities, allocating resources, and assuring explicit documentation for the required project activities.

Question to ponder about pursuing milestones: Suppose you are 65 years old now. Would you embark on a personal project whose end result is not to be realized for decades to come? Why or why not? Consider the incremental gratification of accomplishing milestone along the way. Consider the stages of activity sequencing for any project, spanning the cycle of planning, organizing, activity sequencing, project scheduling, tracking, and control. The cycle is repeated again and again such that the outputs of the control stage are used in subsequent planning functions.

CHAPTER SIX

Work Breakdown Structure

Divide and conquer works for getting things done. Work Breakdown Structure (WBS) refers to the itemization of a project for planning, scheduling, and control purposes. The eventual goal is specified at the top of the WBS diagram, which may also be viewed as the Project Outline. It presents the inherent components of a project in a structured block diagram or interrelationship flow chart. WBS shows the relative hierarchies of parts (phases, segments, milestone, etc.) of the project. The purpose of constructing a WBS is to analyze the elemental components of the project in detail. If a project is properly designed through the application of WBS at the project planning stage, it becomes easier to estimate cost and time requirements of the project. Project control is also enhanced by the ability to identify how components of the project link together. Tasks that are contained in the WBS collectively describe the overall project goal.

Overall project planning and control can be improved by using a WBS approach. A large project may be broken down into smaller sub-projects that may, in turn, be systematically broken down into task groups. Thus, WBS permits the implementation of a "divide and conquer" concept for project control.

In the WBS design, the overall goal is at the top of the structure, followed by all the sub-elements that lead up to the goal. Individual components in a WBS are referred to as WBS elements, and the hierarchy of each is designated by a Level identifier. Elements at the same level of subdivision are said to be of the same WBS level. Descending levels provide increasingly detailed definition of project tasks. The complexity of a project and the degree of control desired determine the number of levels in the WBS. Each component is successively broken down into smaller details at lower levels. The process may continue until specific project activities are noted on the WBS diagram.

In effect, the structure of the WBS looks very much like an organizational chart. The basic approach for preparing a WBS is as follows:

Level 1 WBS
This contains only the final goal of the project. This item should be identifiable directly as an organizational budget item.

Level 2 WBS
This level contains the major sub-sections of the project. These sub-sections are usually identified by their contiguous location or by their related purposes.

Level 3 WBS
Level 3 of the WBS structure contains definable components of the level 2 sub-sections. In technical terms, this may be referred to as the finite element level of the project.

Subsequent levels of WBS are constructed in more specific details depending on the span of control desired. If a complete WBS becomes too crowded, separate WBS layouts may be drawn for the Level 2 components. A statement of work (SOW) or WBS summary should accompany the WBS. The SOW is a narrative of the work to be done. It should include the objectives of the work, its scope, resource requirements, tentative due date, feasibility statements, and so on. A good analysis of the WBS structure will make it easier to perform resource requirement analysis.

Project Organization Chart

Along with work breakdown structure and project planning, a project organization chart must be developed. Even if not drawn out graphically, the chart must be developed, at least conceptually, to show where each person or group belongs in the project structure. There are many alternate forms of project organization chart. Before selecting an organizational structure, the project team should assess the nature of the job to be performed and its requirements.

The organization structure may be defined in terms of functional specializations, departmental proximity, standard management boundaries, operational relationships, or product requirements. In personal projects, the organization structure may be informal and selected based on convenience. It is important to communicate the organizational chart to all those involved in the project.

Traditional Formal Organization Structures

Many organizations use the traditional formal or classical organization structures, which show hierarchical relationships between individuals or teams of individuals. Traditional formal organizational structures are effective in service enterprises because groups with similar functional responsibilities are clustered at the same level of the structure. A formal organizational structure represents the officially sanctioned structure of a functional area. An informal organizational structure, on the other hand, develops when people organize themselves in an unofficial way to accomplish a project objective. The informal organization is often very subtle in that not everyone in the organization is aware of its existence. Both formal and informal organizations exist within every project. Positive characteristics of the traditional formal organizational structure include the following:

- Availability of broad manpower base
- Identifiable technical line of control
- Grouping of specialists to share technical knowledge
- Collective line of responsibility
- Possibility of assigning personnel to several different projects
- Clear hierarchy for supervision
- Continuity and consistency of functional disciplines
- Possibility for the establishment of departmental policies, procedures, and missions.

However, the traditional formal structure does have some negative characteristics as summarized below:

- No one individual is directly responsible for the total project
- Project-oriented planning may be impeded
- There may not be a clear line of reporting up from the lower levels
- Coordination is complex
- A higher level of cooperation is required between adjacent levels
- The strongest functional group may wrongfully claim project authority.

Functional Organization

The most common type of formal organization is known as the functional organization, whereby people are organized into groups dedicated to particular functions. Depending on the size and the type of auxiliary activities involved, several minor, but supporting, functional units can be developed for a project. Projects that are organized along functional lines normally reside in a specific department or area of specialization. The project home office or headquarters is located in the specific functional department. The advantages of a functional organization structure are presented below:

- Improved accountability
- Discernible lines of control
- Flexibility in manpower utilization
- Enhanced comradeship of technical staff
- Improved productivity of specially skilled personnel
- Potential for staff advancement along functional path
- Ability of the home office to serve as a refuge for project problems.

The disadvantages of a functional organization structure include:

- Potential division of attention between project goals and regular functions
- Conflict between project objectives and regular functions
- Poor coordination similar project responsibilities
- Unreceptive attitudes on the part of the surrogate department
- Multiple layers of management
- Lack of concentrated effort.

Product Organization

Another approach to organizing a project is to use the end product or goal of the project as the determining factor for personnel structure. This is often referred to as pure project organization or simply project organization. The project is set up as a unique entity within the parent organization. It has its own dedicated technical staff and administration. It is linked to the rest of the system through progress reports, organizational policies, procedures, and funding. The interface between product-organized projects and other elements of the organization may be strict or liberal, depending on the organization.

The product organization is common in industries that have multiple product lines. Unlike the functional, the product organization decentralizes functions. It creates a unit consisting of specialized skills around a given project or product. Sometimes referred to as a team, task force, or product group, the product organization is common in public, research, and manufacturing organizations where specially organized and designated groups are assigned specific functions. A major advantage of the product organization is that it gives the project members a feeling of dedication to and identification with a particular goal.

A possible shortcoming of the product organization is the requirement that the product group be sufficiently funded to be able to stand alone. The product group may be viewed as an ad hoc unit that is formed for the purpose of a specific goal. The personnel involved in the project are dedicated to the particular mission at hand. At the conclusion of the mission, they may be reassigned to other projects. Product organization can facilitate the most diverse and flexible grouping of project participants. It has the following advantages:

- Simplicity of structure
- Unity of project purpose
- Localization of project failures
- Condensed and focused communication lines
- Full authority of the project manager
- Quicker decisions due to centralized authority
- Skill development due to project specialization
- Improved motivation, commitment, and concentration
- Flexibility in determining time, cost, performance trade-offs
- Project team's reporting directly to one project manager or boss,
- Ability of individuals to acquire and maintain expertise on a given project.

The disadvantages of product organization are:

- Narrow view on the part of project personnel (as opposed to a global organizational view)
- Mutually exclusive allocation of resources (one worker to one project)
- Duplication of efforts on different but similar projects
- Monopoly of organizational resources
- Worker concern about life after the project
- Reduced skill diversification.

One other disadvantage of the product organization is the difficulty supervisors have in assessing the technical competence of individual team members. Since managers are leading people in fields foreign to them, it is difficult for them to assess technical capability. Many major organizations have this problem. Those who can talk a good game and give good presentations are often viewed by management as knowledgeable, regardless of their true technical capabilities.

Matrix Organization Structure

The matrix organization is a frequently-used organization structure in industry. It is used where there is multiple managerial accountability and responsibility for a project. It combines the advantages of the traditional structure and the product organization structure. The hybrid configuration of the matrix structure facilitates maximum resource utilization and increased performance within time, cost, and performance constraints. There are usually two chains of command involving both horizontal and vertical reporting lines. The horizontal line deals with the functional line of responsibility while the vertical line deals with the project line of responsibility.

Advantages of matrix organization include the following:

- Good team interaction

- Consolidation of objectives
- Multilateral flow of information
- Lateral mobility for job advancement
- Individuals have an opportunity to work on a variety of projects
- Efficient sharing and utilization of resources
- Reduced project cost due to sharing of personnel
- Continuity of functions after project completion
- Stimulating interactions with other functional teams
- Functional lines rally to support the project efforts
- Each person has a "home" office after project completion
- Company knowledge base is equally available to all projects.

Some of the disadvantages of matrix organization are summarized below:

- Matrix response time may be slow for fast-paced projects
- Each project organization operates independently
- Overhead cost due to additional lines of command
- Potential conflict of project priorities
- Problems inherent in having multiple bosses
- Complexity of the structure.

Traditionally, industrial projects are conducted in serial functional implementations such as R&D, engineering, manufacturing, and marketing. At each stage, unique specifications and work patterns may be used without consulting the preceding and succeeding phases. The consequence is that the end product may not possess the original intended characteristics. For example, the first project in the series might involve the production of one component while the subsequent projects might involve the production of other components. The composite product may not achieve the desired performance because the components were not designed and produced from a unified point of view. The major appeal of matrix organization is that it attempts to provide synergy within groups in an organization.

Project Feasibility Analysis

The feasibility of a project can be ascertained in terms of technical factors, economic factors, or both. A feasibility study is documented with a report showing all the ramifications of the project and should be broken down into the following categories.

Technical feasibility: "Technical feasibility" refers to the ability of the process to take advantage of the current state of the technology in pursuing further improvement. The technical capability of the personnel as well as the capability of the available technology should be considered.

Managerial feasibility: Managerial feasibility involves the capability of the infrastructure of a process to achieve and sustain process improvement. Management support, employee involvement, and commitment are key elements required to ascertain managerial feasibility.

Economic feasibility: This involves the ability of the proposed project to generate economic benefits. A benefit-cost analysis and a breakeven analysis are important aspects of evaluating the economic feasibility of new industrial projects. The tangible and intangible aspects of a project should be translated into economic terms to facilitate a consistent basis for evaluation.

Financial feasibility: Financial feasibility should be distinguished from economic feasibility. Financial feasibility involves the capability of the project organization to raise the appropriate funds needed to implement the proposed project. Project financing can be a major obstacle in large multi-party projects because of the level of capital required. Loan availability, credit worthiness, equity, and loan schedule are important aspects of financial feasibility analysis.

Cultural feasibility: Cultural feasibility deals with the compatibility of the proposed project with the cultural setup of the project environment. In labor-intensive projects, planned functions must be integrated with the local cultural practices and beliefs. For example, religious beliefs may influence what an individual is willing to do or not do.

Social feasibility: Social feasibility addresses the influences that a proposed project may have on the social system in the project environment. The ambient social structure may be such that certain categories of workers may be in short supply or nonexistent. The effect of the project on the social status of the project participants must be assessed to ensure compatibility. It should be recognized that workers in certain industries may have certain status symbols within the society.

Safety feasibility: Safety feasibility is another important aspect that should be considered in project planning. Safety feasibility refers to an analysis of whether the project is capable of being implemented and operated safely with minimal adverse effects on the environment. Unfortunately, environmental impact assessment is often not adequately addressed in complex projects. As an example, the North America Free Trade Agreement (NAFTA) between the U.S., Canada, and Mexico was temporarily suspended in 1993 because of the legal consideration of the potential environmental impacts of the projects to be undertaken under the agreement.

Political feasibility: A politically feasible project may be referred to as a "politically correct project." Political considerations often dictate the direction for a proposed project. This is particularly true for large projects with national visibility that may have significant government inputs and political implications. For example, political necessity may be a source of support for a project regardless of the project's merits. On the other hand, worthy projects may face insurmountable opposition simply because of political factors. Political feasibility analysis requires an evaluation of the compatibility of project goals with the prevailing goals of the political system.

<u>Family feasibility</u>: As long as we, as human beings, belong within some family setting, whether immediate family or extended relatives, family feasibility should be one of the dimensions of the overall feasibility of a project. This is not normally addressed in conventional project feasibility analysis. But it is important enough to be included as an explicit requirement. For example, a decision to move from one city to another for the purpose of starting a new corporate job should be made with respect to family needs, desires, and preferences.

<u>Project Need analysis</u>: This indicates recognition of a need for the project. The need may affect the organization itself, another organization, the public, or the government. A preliminary study is conducted to confirm and evaluate the need. A proposal of how the need may be satisfied is then made. Pertinent questions that should be asked include the following:

- Is the need significant enough to justify the proposed project?
- Will the need still exist by the time the project is completed?
- What are alternate means of satisfying the need?
- What are the economic, social, environmental, and political impacts of the need?

It is essential to identify and resolve conflicts in project planning early before resources are committed to work elements that do not add value to the final goal of a project.

CHAPTER SEVEN

Communication, Cooperation, and Coordination

Communication is the root of everything else, even in a kitchen. Communication, cooperation, and coordination are essential for getting things done in the kitchen, even where no other participants are involved. It is often said that one should listen to the inner voice. Well, that is, indeed, an example of self-communication. Similarly, self-awareness is an example of self-cooperation. Furthermore, being organized means being well coordinated.

Organizations thrive by investing in the three primary resources as outlined below:

- the **people** who do the work,
- the **tools** that the people use to do the work,
- and the **process** that governs the work that the people do.

Of the three, investing in people is the easiest thing an organization can do and we should do it whenever we have an opportunity. The Triple C model, which advocates integrated communication, cooperation, and coordination, incorporates the qualitative (human) aspects of a project into the overall project requirements.

The Triple C model is effective for project control. The model states that project management can be enhanced by implementing it within the integrated functions summarized below:

- Communication
- Cooperation
- Coordination

The Triple C model facilitates a systematic approach to project planning, organizing, scheduling, and control. The Triple C model can be implemented for project planning, scheduling and control purposes for any type of project. Each project element requires effective communication, sustainable cooperation, and adaptive coordination.

The basic questions of what, who, why, how, where, and when revolve around the Triple C model. It highlights what must be done and when. It can also help to identify the resources (personnel, equipment, facilities, etc.) required for each effort through communication and coordination processes. It points out important questions such as the following:

- Does each project participant know what the objective is?
- Does each participant know his or her role in achieving the objective?
- What obstacles may prevent a participant from playing his or her role effectively?

Triple C can mitigate disparity between idea and practice because it explicitly solicits information about the critical aspects of a project. The written communication requirement of the Triple C approach helps to document crucial information needed for project control later on.

Project Communication

Communication makes is possible for people to work together. The communication function in any project effort involves making all those concerned become aware of project requirements and progress. Those who will be affected by the project directly or indirectly, as direct participants or as beneficiaries, should be informed as appropriate regarding the following:

- Scope of the project
- Personnel contribution required
- Expected cost and merits of the project
- Project organization and implementation plan
- Potential adverse effects if the project should fail
- Alternatives, if any, for achieving the project goal
- Potential direct and indirect benefits of the project

The communication channel must be kept open throughout the project life cycle. In addition to internal communication, appropriate external sources should also be consulted. The project manager must

- Exude commitment to the project
- Utilize the communication responsibility matrix
- Facilitate multi-channel communication interfaces
- Identify internal and external communication needs
- Resolve organizational and communication hierarchies
- Encourage both formal and informal communication links

Types of Communication

- Verbal
- Written
- Body language
- Visual tools (e.g., graphical tools)

- Sensual (Use of all five senses: sight, smell, touch, taste, hearing:-olfactory, tactile, auditory)
- Simplex (unidirectional)
- Half-duplex (bi-directional with time lag)
- Full-duplex (real-time dialogue)
- One-on-one
- One-to-many
- Many-to-one

Project Cooperation

The cooperation of the project personnel must be explicitly elicited. Merely voicing consent for a project is not enough assurance of full cooperation. The participants and beneficiaries of the project must be convinced of the merits of the project. Some of the factors that influence cooperation in a project environment include personnel requirements, resource requirements, budget limitations, past experiences, conflicting priorities, and lack of uniform organizational support. A structured approach to seeking cooperation should clarify the following:

- Cooperative efforts required
- Precedents for future projects
- Implication of lack of cooperation
- Criticality of cooperation to project success
- Organizational impact of cooperation
- Time frame involved in the project
- Rewards of good cooperation

Cooperation is a basic virtue of human interaction. More projects fail due to a lack of cooperation and commitment than any other project factors. To secure and retain the cooperation of project participants, you must elicit a positive first reaction to the project. The most positive aspects of a project should be the first items of project communication.

For project management, there are different types of cooperation that should be understood.

Functional cooperation: This is cooperation induced by the nature of the functional relationship between two groups. The two groups may be required to perform related functions that can only be accomplished through mutual cooperation.

Social cooperation: As the joint apples to the right suggest, *if we work together, we will grow together.* Social cooperation implies collaboration to pursue a common goal. This is the type of cooperation effected by the social relationship between two groups. The prevailing social relationship motivates cooperation that may be useful in getting project work done. Thus, everyone succeeds as a part of the group.

Legal cooperation: Legal cooperation is the type of cooperation that is imposed through some authoritative requirement. In this case, the participants may have no choice other than to cooperate.

Administrative cooperation: This is cooperation brought on by administrative requirements that make it imperative that two groups work together on a common goal.

Associative cooperation: This type of cooperation may also be referred to as collegiality. The level of cooperation is determined by the association that exists between two groups.

Proximity cooperation: Cooperation due to the fact that two groups are geographically close is referred to as proximity cooperation. Being close makes it imperative that the two groups work together.

Dependency cooperation: This is cooperation caused by the fact that one group depends on another group for some important aspect. Such dependency is usually of a mutual two-way nature. One group depends on the other for one thing while the latter group depends on the former for some other thing.

Imposed cooperation: In this type of cooperation, external agents must be employed to induced cooperation between two groups. This is applicable for cases where the two groups have no natural reason to cooperate. This is where the approaches presented earlier for seeking cooperation can became very useful.

Lateral cooperation: Lateral cooperation involves cooperation with peers and immediate associates. Lateral cooperation is often easy to achieve because existing lateral relationships create an environment that is conducive for project cooperation.

Vertical cooperation: Vertical or hierarchical cooperation refers to cooperation that is implied by the hierarchical structure of the project. For example, subordinates are expected to cooperate with their vertical superiors.

Whichever type of cooperation is available in a project environment; the cooperative forces should be channeled toward achieving project goals. Documentation of the prevailing level of cooperation is useful for winning further support for a project. Clarification of project priorities will facilitate personnel cooperation. Relative priorities of multiple projects should be specified so that a priority to all groups within the organization. One of the best times to seek and obtain cooperation is during holiday periods when most people are in festive and receptive mood. Some guidelines for securing cooperation for most projects are

- Establish achievable goals for the project.
- Clearly outline the individual commitments required.
- Integrate project priorities with existing priorities.
- Eliminate the fear of job loss due to industrialization.
- Anticipate and eliminate potential sources of conflict.
- Use an open-door policy to address project grievances.
- Remove skepticism by documenting the merits of the project.

Types of Cooperation

Cooperation falls in several different categories. Some have physical sources, some have emotional sources, and some have psychological sources. The most common categories of cooperation include the following:

- Proximity
- Functional
- Professional
- Social
- Romantic
- Power influence
- Authority influence
- Hierarchical
- Lateral
- Cooperation by intimidation
- Cooperation by enticement

Project Coordination

After communication and cooperation functions have successfully been initiated, the efforts of the project personnel must be coordinated. Coordination facilitates harmonious organization of project efforts. The construction of a responsibility chart can be very helpful at this stage. A responsibility chart is a matrix consisting of columns of individual or functional departments and rows of required actions. Cells within the matrix are filled with relationship codes that indicate who is responsible for what. The matrix helps avoid neglecting crucial communication requirements and obligations. It can help resolve questions such as

- Who is to do what?
- How long will it take?
- Who is to inform whom of what?

- Whose approval is needed for what?
- Who is responsible for which results?
- What personnel interfaces are required?
- What support is needed from whom and when?

Types of Coordination

- Teaming
- Delegation
- Supervision
- Partnership
- Token-passing
- Baton hand-off

Through communication, cooperation, and coordination, we can offer a ***helping hand*** to our colleagues, friends, and team members so as to get our objectives accomplished. One good turn deserves another. As we succeed together with one project, so we shall succeed with another mutual project.

CHAPTER EIGHT

Applying 5S Methodology in the Kitchen

An organized and timely execution of kitchen chores is a great passion for us. We want others to experience and enjoy the joy of smooth kitchen operations. That is our motivation for embarking on this particular book project. The 5S methodology, which is frequently used in business and industry, is directly applicable in kitchen project management. Planning, organizing, and coordinating constitute the foundation for successful execution of kitchen projects. The 5S methodology is directly relevant for such pursuits.

5S is a Japanese methodology developed for efficient and effective management of production facilities. The 5S represent the following Japanese words:

1. *Seiri*
2. *Seiton*
3. *Seiso*

4. *Seiketsu*
5. *shitsuke*

These words translate to the following English words:

1. Sort
2. Set in Order
3. Shine
4. Standardize
5. Sustain

The utilization of 5S can help organize the kitchen. 5S advocates having "a place for everything and everything is in its place." The five main levels for 5S are explained below.

- **Sort:** Identify and eliminate materials that do not belong. This is to sort out any necessary and unnecessary items. Many items can be disposed of if they are not needed. This will remove waste, create a safer work area, gain space, and help visualize the process easier. It is important to sort through the entire area, not leaving anything out. The removal of items should be discussed with all personnel involved. Items that cannot be removed immediately should be tagged.
- **Sweep:** Clean the area so that it looks like new. This is essential for kitchen project management. Cleaning as you go along in the kitchen will ensure that you end up with a clean kitchen in the end, thus avoiding the overwhelming chore of massive cleaning at the end. Sweep is to keep the area clean on a continuous basis. Sweeping prevents the area from getting dirty in the first place so there is no need to clean it up after the fact. A clean work place indicates a place that has high standards of quality and good process controls. Sweeping should eliminate dirt, build pride in work areas, and build value in equipment.
- **Straighten:** Have a place for everything and everything in its place. Arranging all necessary items is the first step. This will

visually show what is required and show what is in and out of its place. This helps efficiency when looking for a particular item by saving time and having shorter travel distances. The things that are used together should be kept together. Labels, floor markings, signs, tape, and shadowed outlines can be used for this process. Items to be shared can be kept at a central location to eliminate excess items. The best kitchens are the best organized. Straightening things out implies getting things organized in the kitchen.

- **Schedule:** Assign responsibilities and due dates to actions. Scheduling maintains guidelines of sorting, sweeping, and straightening. It prevents regressing back to unclean or disorganized environments. Scheduling returns items where they belong and eliminates the need for "special clean-up acts" by cleaning routinely. Scheduling normally entails checklists and schedules to continually improve neatness.
- **Sustain:** Establishing ways to ensure future compliance of manufacturing or process improvements. Sustaining maintains discipline and ensures practicing of proper processes until it seems like it is a way of life. Training is key to sustaining and involvement of all parties is necessary. Commitment towards housekeeping is mandated from management for this process to be successful.

The benefits of 5S are:

- A cleaner and safer workplace
- Providing customer satisfaction by promoting a more organized pursuit
- Increased quality, productivity, and effectiveness

Kaizen (Kai-Zen) events normally are key processes for starting a 5S project.

Kai - means to break apart or to disassemble so that one can begin to understand

Zen - means to improve

This is directly applicable for the project work breakdown structure, in which complexity is divided to be conquered.

A Kaizen process focuses on an improvement objective to break apart the process into its basic elements in order to understand it, identify the waste, create improvement ideas, and eliminate the waste identified.

The basic philosophy of an operational Kaizen is to manufacture products safely, manufacture products when they are needed and produce products that are needed with the proper quantity needed. The objectives are to reduce cycle time and lead time. Kaizen will also increase productivity, reduce WIP, eliminate defects, enhance capacity, increase flexibility, improve layout, sand establish visual management and measures.

Kaizen will increase productivity by viewing operator cycle time, eliminating waste, balancing workloads, utilizing value added tasks, and producing to demand. Kaizen will reduce WIP by determining needed and unneeded inventory. Like production outputs will be grouped together to balance production. Set-up times can be reduced; batches of outputs can be transported in smaller quantities. Preventative maintenance schedules can be established along with quality stability. Kaizen will eliminate defects by asking why five or more times, reducing inventory so that improper manufacturing operations are caught directly after processing, performing under stable and similar work conditions, and devising mistake-proofing devices. Kaizen will enhance capacity and increase flexibility by finding bottlenecks in humans and machines. Waste is identified and eliminated in humans and machines. Layouts can be improved by gaining flexibility with respect to the flow of objects, people, and machines. Layouts need to be safe, clean, able to incur preventative maintenance regularly, have minimal staffing, and have limited transportation times. Shortened walking distance and movement should be sought after when creating a layout. Work should enter and exit the cell at the same place. There should be communication between all members within the cell and the work balance should be even. The workers should be able to help each other out if needed.

Kaizen can be segregated into two main points: Equipment vs. Operational. Equipment based improvements cost money, take time, have major modifications, and are often not linked to cost savings. Operational-based improvements do the following:

- Change standard operating procedures
- Change positions of layouts, tools, equipment
- Simplify tools by adding chutes, knock out devices, levers
- Improve equipment without drastically modifying
- Cost little or no money and focuses on cost reduction

Materials are another part of Kaizen focuses. Materials are the analogy for ingredients in a kitchen project management. It focuses on one piece of equipment or one set of flows, synchronized movements, shortened transfer distances, movement of inventory into designated or finished states, and keeps a necessary buffer between flows while not disturbing another flow.

Quality is always a part of Kaizen or Lean and Six Sigma. Defects are to be reduced, flows are to be improved, and processes are to be stream lined.

Lastly, Safety and Environments should always be considered during Kaizen. As operations or layouts are changed, safety and environment should always be thought about. Safety and Environment comes before any type of cost savings or productivity increases. The consideration of "safety" leads to the advent of expanding 5S to 6S.

There are ten basic rules when thinking about Kaizen:

1. Thinking "outside the box", no new idea should be a bad idea.
2. How it can be done versus how it cannot be done.
3. No excuses, question existing practices.

4. Perfection may not come right away, improvements need to be made first.
5. Mistakes should be corrected as soon as possible.
6. Quick and Simple ideas should be done for Kaizen, not spending a great amount of money.
7. As hard as the process may be, it finds intelligence in other people's ideas.
8. Ask "Why?" at least 5 times to find root causes.
9. Consult more than one person to find a true solution.
10. Kaizen ideas are ever-lasting.

Visual management and measures can help with successful layouts. The visual management can consist of bins, cards, tags, signals, lights, alarms, and any type of signaling mechanisms. The levels of visual systems are the following:

Visual indicators – Passive Information such as signs, maps, and displays

Visual signals – Assertive Information such as alarms or lights

Visual controls – Aggressive Information such as size, weight, width, or length

Visual guarantees – Assured Information such as sensors, guides, locators

Developing visual management systems includes normal housekeeping such as 5S.

CHAPTER NINE

Applying PDCA Methodology
in the Kitchen

Process improvement is as important in the kitchen as it is in the corporate World. The Plan-Do-Check-Act (PDCA) methodology is a common tool for continuous process improvement. The best chefs are always striving to do better not only in their culinary act, but also in the management of their cooking pursuits, which means that they embrace continuous process improvement.

PDCA (Plan-Do-Check-Act) is a recursive and iterative methodology for continually assessing and improving operations. Kitchen operations are not exempt from this categorization. So, PDCA technique is applicable in the kitchen. The application of PDCA helps to diagnose problems early so that resolution strategies can be instituted. PDCA evolved out of the scientific work-management research of Dr W. Edwards Deming. Dr. Deming is reputed to be the originator of modern quality control along with some Japanese contemporaries. PDCA requires pursuing improvements in small increments, which are later developed into organization-wide implementations. The stages or PDCA are described below:

Plan

- Identify the problem
- Collect pertinent data
- Understand the problem's root cause.
- Develop hypotheses about what the problems may be.
- Decide which hypothesis to test.

"Plan" is carried out in three steps. The first step is the identification of the problem. The second step is an analysis of this problem. The third step is the development of an experiment to test it. Some of the things to consider during this process include the following:

Problem Identification

- Is this the right problem to work on?
- Is this problem important and impactful for the organization?
- Who does the problem affect and what is the potential impact of solving it?

Problem Analysis

- What is the requisite information needed to fully understand the problem and its root cause?
- What data do we already have related to the problem? What data do we need to collect?
- Who should be enlisted or interviewed to better understand the problem?
- After understanding the problem, is it feasible to solve it? Will the solution be economical and practical?

- Developing an Experiment
- What are some viable solutions?
- Who will be involved in the process and who will be responsible for it?
- What is the expected outcome of the experiment and how can we measure performance?
- What are the resources necessary to run a small-scale experiment?
- How will the results from the small-scale experiment translate to a full-fledged implementation?

Do

- Develop and implement a solution.
- Decide a measurement to gauge its effectiveness.
- Test the potential solution.
- Measure the results.

The "Do" stage is where we test the proposed solutions or changes. Ideally, this should be carried out in small-scale studies. Small-scale experiments allow us to learn quickly, adjust as needed, and are typically less expensive to undertake. Make sure that you measure the performance and collect the data necessary to make an evaluation later on.

Check

- Confirm the results through before-and-after data comparison.
- Study the result and measure effectiveness.
- Decide whether the hypothesis is supported or not.

In Check stage, review the experiment, analyze the results, and identify what has been learned. Pertinent questions include:

- Did the implementation of the change achieve the desired results?

- What did not work?
- What was learned from the implementation?
- Is there enough data to show that the change was effective?
- Do you need to run another experiment?
- How does the small-scale experiment measure up to the larger picture?
- Is the proposed solution still viable and practical?

Act

- Document the results.
- Communicate the process changes to others.
- Make recommendations for the future PDCA cycles.
- If the solution was successful, implement it.
- If not, tackle the next problem and repeat the PDCA cycle again.

In the Act stage, we will take action based on what was learned in the study. If the change did not work, go through the cycle again with a different plan. If successful, incorporate into wider changes. Use what has been learned to plan new improvements and start the cycle again. If the plan worked, you need to standardize the process and implement it widely. Pertinent questions for the Act stage include the following:

- What resources are needed to implement the solution company-wide?
- What kind of training is needed for full implementation of the improvement?
- How can the change be maintained and sustained?
- How can we measure and monitor the impact of the solution?
- What are some other areas of improvement?
- How can we use what we have learned in this experiment to devise other experiments?

The PDCA Cycle provides a framework and structure for identifying improvement opportunities and evaluating them objectively. The PDCA process supports both the principles and practice of continuous improvement and Kaizen. Kaizen focuses on applying small, daily changes that result in major improvements over time.

Kaizen basically means "Take apart and make better."

In this context, we can use the analogy of the mathematics of "finite element analysis."

It is from the intricate details that one can identify what can be easily improved. In order words, you have a better grasp of what has been "taken apart" so that the elements can be rebuilt "better" and more structurally linked.

The Kaizen approach also helps to get to the root of problems. If done well, Kaizen can help preempt production problems. There is always room for improvement. It is when something is disassembled that it can be reconfigured to be better. A simple example of what we can call the "Kaizen flow" is provided below:

Manufacturing System - Process -Subprocess -
Task - Production Activity.

This facilitates a bottom-up approach to achieving improvements in a manufacturing environment. For a kitchen project management application of Kaizen, we can embed additional elements of interest into the flow. An analogical flow might look like the following:

Recipe - Ingredients - Preparation - Kitchen
utensils placement - Cook

Kaizen methods can be used to create a better kitchen environment while still achieving the desired culinary outputs.

CHAPTER TEN

Project Management Template for the Kitchen

In this chapter, the preceding general guidelines for project management are summarized into a condensed template for a quick reference. Where applicable, analogical examples and descriptions are offered for the kitchen environment.

Pots and pans can get in the way of good organization in the kitchen. So, it is essential to get proactively organized. Project management is a good way to get a kitchen organized and functioning as expected. It is not only about the food coming out of the kitchen. It is also about the process of getting the food prepared. A disorganized kitchen can lead to "dis-flavoring" outputs from the kitchen. This is an area that is often neglected in food preparation endeavors. Kitchen projects should be managed just like any other project. A clean slate provides a clean output. An organized kitchen provides a well-organized culinary output.

Basic Guidelines for an Organized Kitchen

To avoid a disorganized kitchen, do the following:

- Always make a list of what needs to be done, no matter how many times you have gone through the routine before. Each day is different in terms of the moods and methods of the day. So, a new list for each day can be effective in averting kitchen debacles.
- Store things where they normally belong, which, by the way, should be close to the point of use.
- Organize small items in transparent labeled containers for ease of access and movement.
- Clean as you go to avoid an overwhelming pile of soiled items at the end. Little increments of cleaning ensure that everything gets a proper attention at the right time.
- Group similar items to form a ready coalition of kitchen tools.
- Store most frequently-used items in the most accessible places.
- Declutter the kitchen periodically. The more frequently this is done, the more control you will have over your kitchen assets.
- Get rid of duplicative items, unless they are needed for redundancy and flexibility of size and effectiveness.
- Store items at convenient and reachable heights to accommodate the reach of different users.
- Have a small step stool near the kitchen to avoid the temptation of unsafe above-head reach and stretch for needed items.
- Items that don't belong in the kitchen have no place in the kitchen. Move them!

The tools and techniques of project management are directly applicable to large-scale cooking projects. In this case, we are focusing on large-scale cooking for social events rather than institutional undertakings, like restaurants. A project is conventionally defined as "a unique one-of-a-kind endeavor with a definite beginning and a definite end." Large-scale cooking project do, indeed, have all the makings of a conventional project and should be managed accordingly. A project is constituted to achieve one or more of the following three outputs:

1. Produce a physical product
2. Provide a certain service
3. Generate a desired result

A cooking project meets all three of the above output categories. Cooking produces a physical consumable product in terms of menu items. Cooking, particularly through a catering business, provides a service in terms helping to meet the needs of the client to provide food for guests and visitors. Cooking, if done properly, will generate the desired result of quenching hunger while satisfying the palate. Project management is an integral part of human existence and a key factor in achieving operational excellence in technical, professional, and domestic functions. For large-scale cooking projects, the proof of project management pudding is in what comes out of the kitchen.

Many, many people in the population are homemakers. Homemakers are not necessarily stay-at-home moms. We see more and more, working moms and dads also managing home projects. Kitchen-based projects are particularly common. This makes it imperative to apply project management tools and techniques in the kitchen to save time and improve the cooking process. In order to get the best output of your kitchen, you must manage the kitchen enterprise just as you would manage any personal or professional project.

Based on the definition of homemakers utilized by the U.S. Census Bureau, homemakers are individuals who perform duties or "projects" at home that include home-keeping, cooking, making beds, doing laundry, washing dishes, dusting, assembling products, installing gadgets, managing electronics, monitoring utilities, organizing garages, shoveling snow, decorating, and making household repairs. Homemakers also advise families, provide healthcare, and mete out discipline to kids. These are a whole lot of projects (small or big, easy or difficult, simple or complex) that can be found around the home. Each and every one of them needs help from project management.

In his professional project management textbook, Deji defines project management as "the process of managing, allocating, and timing resources to accomplish objectives in an efficient and expeditious manner."

Steps of Project Management: The objectives of a project may be stated in terms of time (schedule), performance (quality), or cost (budget). Time is often the most critical aspect of managing any project. Time must be managed concurrently with all other important aspects of any project, particularly in an academic setting. Project management covers the basic stages listed below:

1. Initiation
2. Planning
3. Execution
4. Tracking and Control
5. Closure

The stages are often contracted or expanded based on the needs of the specific project. They can also overlap based on prevailing project scenarios. For example, tracking and control often occur concurrently with project execution. Embedded within execution is the function of activity scheduling. If contracted, the list of stages may include only Planning, Organizing, Scheduling, and Control. In this case, closure is seen as a control action. If expanded, the list may include additional explicit stages such as Conceptualization, Scoping, Resource Allocation, and Reporting.

Kitchen Project Initiation

What is worth doing is worth doing well. What is worth doing well is worth initiating properly. The proper initiation of a kitchen project can pave the way for a good culinary output devoid of stressful actions and reactions. In the first stage of the project lifecycle, the scope of the project is defined along with the approach to be taken to deliver the desired results. The project manager and project team are appointed based on skills, experience, and relevance. The process of organizing the project is often carried out as a bridge or overlap between initiation and planning. The most common tools used in the initiation stage are Project Charter, Business Plan, Project Framework, Overview, Process Mapping, Business Case Justification, and Milestone Reviews. Project initiation normally takes place after problem identification and project definition.

Kitchen Project Planning

A chaotic kitchen can develop if no proper planning has been put in place. The second stage of the project lifecycle includes a detailed identification and assignment of tasks making up the project. It should also include a risk analysis and a definition of criteria for the successful completion of each deliverable. During planning, the management process is defined, stakeholders are identified, reporting frequency is established, and communication channels are agreed upon. The most common tools used in the planning stage are Brainstorming, Business Plan, Process Mapping, and Milestones Reviews.

For kitchen planning purpose, what you can do in advance (before the actual cooking starts), should be done in advance.

What can be done in parallel (while the cooking is going on) should be done concurrently.

Kitchen Project Control

A kitchen project without control steps will end in a disaster. The most important issue in the execution and control stages of the project lifecycle involves ensuring that tasks are executed expeditiously in accordance with the project plan, which is always subject to re-planning. Tracking is an implicit component and prerequisite for project control. For projects that are organized for producing physical products, a design resulting in a specific set of product requirements is created. The integrity of the product is assured through prototypes, validation, verification, and testing. As the execution phase progresses, groups across the organization become progressively involved in the realization of the project objectives. The most common tools or methodologies used in the execution stage include Risk Analysis, Balance Scorecards, Business Plan Review, and Milestone Assessment.

Kitchen Project Closure

In the closure stage, the project is phased-out or formally terminated. Every kitchen undertaking should be formally closed, perhaps through a final cleanup. The closure process is often gradual as the project is weaned of resources and personnel are reallocated to other organizational needs. Acceptance of deliverables is an important part of project closure. The closure phase is characterized by a formal project review covering the following components: a formal acceptance of the final product, Weighted Critical Measurements (matching the initial requirements with the final product delivered), thanking and rewarding the participants, documentation of a list of lessons learned, releasing project resources, doing a formal project closure, and project cleanup. Deji does use project management techniques in his kitchen and home projects.

To cook, you must have a kitchen.
To cook well, your kitchen must be well managed. That's the art of it.

The art of cooking comes glaringly across by the way the kitchen is managed. A poorly managed kitchen will translate to poor gastronomic outputs. Cooking should be viewed as an avenue for artistic expression. Your kitchen should be viewed as your arts studio. You would not think of an arts studio without basic tools, paints, canvas, and other "ingredients" of beautiful art. Stock your kitchen so that you won't go wanting in the process of creating your work of kitchen art. Unless you have a Nigerian neighbor, you may not be able to go running through the neighborhood in search of who has a box of salt, a packet of sugar, or a sachet of nutmeg at an odd hour of the evening when your guests are about to arrive.

The battle of watts and lumens looms in the kitchen. A kitchen should be well lighted. A question often comes up regarding using a higher wattage bulb to get more light into a room. To clarify, wattage is a measure of energy consumption while lumens represent a measure of light emission. Thus, a bulb that gives off higher lumens is preferred for getting a room better lit. In general, lower-wattage bulbs tend to be less efficient. Thus, if you want more light, it can be achieved with a larger-wattage bulb compared to using multiple smaller-wattage bulbs.

Project tips for the kitchen

Tips offered in this section can have direct implications on the success of a kitchen project.

- Plan your cooking project and execute the project according to plan.
- Have contingency plans in case things don't go well.
- Always allow enough time for your cooking projects. Quality takes time. A rushed cooking project could become a failed project.
- Manage your kitchen time judiciously. Distractions cost time. Rework also costs time. Preempt accidents and errors that will cost you time in your cooking project.
- For safety reasons, never leave the handle of a pot on the stove hanging over the edge of the stove. Kitchen accidents, even minor ones, cost time in terms of emergency, personal injury, and recovery time.
- Never leave hot food or appliances unattended while cooking. If you are frying, boiling, or broiling food, stay with your ***project***

in the kitchen. Project monitoring and oversight are essential for any successful project.

- Avoid engaging in a kitchen project if you are impaired due to the influence of medication or drugs.
- Keep anything that can catch on fire at least three feet from the stove, toaster oven, burners, or other heat sources.
- Keep the stovetop, burners, and oven clean before, during, and after each cooking project.
- Do not wear loose fitting clothes when you are cooking. A fire hazard can detract from project success.
- If all the stove burners are not in use when you cook, use the back-row burners. This allows for more operational space around the focal point of your project. This also minimizes the risk of a child reaching for any hot stuff on the cooking surface.
- Keep appliance cords coiled, away from the counter edges, and out of reach of children.
- Use oven mitts or pot-holders when carrying hot food.
- Open hot containers from the microwave slowly and away from your face.
- Never use a wet oven mitt, as it presents a scalding risk if the moisture in the mitt is heated.
- Never hold a child while cooking, carrying or drinking hot foods or liquids. Multi-tasking with kid care is a no-no in the kitchen zone.
- In the clean-up stage, do not mix different chemical cleaning agents in order to avoid kitchen disasters, which could create an impediment to project success. For example, mixing bleach and ammonia can generate a chemical reaction, which is not only dangerous, but also disruptive to the flow of the kitchen project.
- To separate two glasses that are stuck together, fill the top glass with ice water; the cold will make the glass molecules contract. While the top glass is still full of ice water, run hot water over the bottom glass, or place it in a few inches of hot water. The higher temperature makes the bottom glass expand. Gently twist the two glasses. They should come apart easily.

Vinegar in the kitchen project

- A mixture of salt and vinegar will clean coffee and tea stains from chinaware.
- Freshen vegetables. Soak wilted vegetables in 2 cups of water and a tablespoon of vinegar.
- Boil better eggs by adding 2 tablespoons water before boiling. Keeps them from cracking.
- Marinating meat in vinegar kills bacteria and tenderizes the meat. Use one-quarter cup vinegar for a two to three-pound roast, marinate overnight, and then cook without draining or rinsing the meat.
- Add herbs to the vinegar when marinating as desired.
- Put vinegar on a cloth and let sit on the back of your kitchen faucet and it removes hard water stains.
- Vinegar can help to dissolve mineral deposits that collect in automatic drip coffee makers. Fill the reservoir with vinegar and run it through a brewing cycle. Rinse thoroughly with water when the cycle is finished. (Be sure to check the owner's manual for specific instructions).
- Brass, copper and pewter will shine if cleaned with the following mixture. Dissolve 1 teaspoon of salt in one (1) cup of distilled vinegar.
- Clean the dishwasher by running a cup of vinegar through the whole cycle once a month to reduce soap build up on the inner mechanisms and on glassware.
- Deodorize the kitchen drain. Pour a cup of vinegar down the drain once a week. Let stand 30 minutes and then flush with cold water.
- Unclog a drain. Pour a handful of baking soda down the drain and add ½ cup of vinegar. Rinse with hot water.
- Eliminate onion odor by rubbing vinegar on your fingers before and after slicing.
- Clean and disinfect wood cutting boards by wiping with full strength vinegar.

- Cut grease and odor on dishes by adding a tablespoon of vinegar to hot soapy water.
- Clean a teapot by boiling a mixture of water and vinegar in it. Wipe away the grime.
- Clean and deodorize the garbage disposal by making vinegar ice cubes and feed them down the disposal. After grinding, run cold water through.
- Clean and deodorize jars. Rinse mayonnaise, peanut butter, and mustard jars with vinegar when empty.
- Get rid of cooking smells by letting a small pot of vinegar and water simmer on the stove.
- Clean the refrigerator by washing with a solution of equal parts water and vinegar.
- Clean stainless steel by wiping with vinegar dampened cloth.
- Clean china and fine glassware by adding a cup of vinegar to a sink of warm water. Gently dip the glass or china in the solution and let dry.
- Get stains out of pots by filling the pots with a solution of three (3) tablespoons of vinegar to a pint of water. Boil until stain loosens and can be washed away.
- Clean food-stained pots and pans by filling the pots and pans with vinegar and let stand for thirty minutes. Then rinse in hot, soapy water.
- Clean the microwave by boiling a solution of ¼ cup of vinegar and 1 cup of water in the microwave. It will loosen splattered on food and deodorize.
- Make buttermilk. Add a tablespoon of vinegar to a cup of milk and let it stand for five (5) minutes to thicken.
- Replace a lemon by substituting ¼ teaspoon of vinegar for 1 teaspoon of lemon juice.
- Firm up gelatin by adding a teaspoon of vinegar for every box of gelatin used. To keep those molded desserts from sagging in the summer heat.
- Prepare fluffier rice by adding a teaspoon of vinegar to the water when it boils.

- Make wine vinegar by mixing two (2) tablespoons of vinegar with 1 teaspoon of dry red wine.
- Debug fresh vegetables by washing them in water with vinegar and salt. Bugs float off.
- Scale fish more easily by rubbing with vinegar five (5) minutes before scaling.
- Prevent soap film on glassware by placing a cup of vinegar on the bottom rack of your dishwasher, run for five minutes, then run though the full cycle.
- The minerals found in foods and water will often leave a dark stain on aluminum utensils. This stain can be easily removed by boiling a solution of 1 tablespoon of distilled vinegar per cup of water in the utensil. Utensils may also be boiled in the solution.
- Unsightly film in small-necked bottles and other containers can be cleaned by pouring vinegar into the bottle and shaking. For tougher stains, add a few tablespoons of rice or sand and shake vigorously. Rinse thoroughly and repeat until clean or determined hopeless.
- After cleaning the bread box, keep it smelling sweet by wiping it down with a cloth moistened in distilled vinegar.
- To eliminate fruit stains from your hands, rub your hands with a little distilled vinegar and wipe with a cloth
- Grease build-up in an oven can be prevented by wiping with a cleaning ran that has been moistened in distilled vinegar and water.
- Formica tops and counters will shine in cleaned with a cloth soaked in distilled vinegar.
- No-wax linoleum will shine better if wiped with a solution of ½ cup of white vinegar in ½ gallon of water.
- Stains on hard-to-clean glass, aluminum, or porcelain utensils may be loosened by boiling in a solution of one-part vinegar to eight parts water. The utensils should then be washed in hot soapy water.

Ginger in the kitchen project

- Ginger up! Ginger can spice up a lot of things with ginger. Ginger is a multi-faceted root not only for cooking, but also for therapeutic applications in the home. Two common applications are for cough/sore throat therapy and relief of indigestion.
- Directions: Scrape off the bark from the root, and cut the remaining root into small, cough-drop-sized pieces. The taste is very strong, and has a spicy flavor. For mild relief, suck the ginger for a light dose of the juice, and for more intensity, bite slightly into the root to squeeze more of the juice out. This is very effective if you feel you are about to cough.
- Ginger also acts as a digestive aid. It can cut through excess mucous, and help relieve an upset stomach. Chew up on the cough-drop ginger pieces and swallow them to relieve indigestion. There is a ginger tea that helps with this, with colds, and with coughing.
- Making Ginger Tea: To make ginger tea, prepare the root the same way it is done for cough drops. Cut the ginger into chunks, and put in a saucepan with a good quantity of filtered or spring water. Slowly cook the brew until about three quarters of the water boils off. This will produce a very spicy tea, which will aid the digestion and even help strengthen the immune system.

Baking soda in the kitchen project

Baking soda is a chemical compound, bicarbonate of soda, that appears as a fine powder. It releases bubbles of carbon dioxide when it interacts with an acid and a liquid. It is most commonly used in baking, where it acts as a leavening agent. It has many different uses in the kitchen. It often works better than many commercially available and expensive products for the same uses.

- Sprinkle baking soda on grease or electrical fire to safely put it out. This also works for car engine fire. Baking soda will also put out fires in clothing, fuel, wood, upholstery and rugs.
- Clean vegetables and fruit with baking soda. Sprinkle in water, soak and rinse the vegetables.
- Wash garbage cans with baking soda to freshen and eliminate odors.
- Oil and grease in clothes stains will wash out better with soda added to the washing water.
- Clean fridge and freezer with dry baking soda sprinkled on a damp cloth and rinse with clear water.
- Deodorize fridge and freezer by putting in an open container of baking soda to absorb odors. Stir and turn over the soda from time to time. Replace every 2 months.
- Wash food and drink containers with baking soda and water.
- Wash marble-topped kitchen cabinet furniture with a solution of three tablespoons of baking soda in one quart of warm water. Let stand awhile and then rinse with clear water.
- Wash out thermos bottles and cooling containers with soda and water to get rid of stale smells.
- To remove stubborn stains from marble or plastic surfaces, scour with a paste of soda and water.
- Wash glass or stainless-steel coffee pots (but not aluminum) in a soda solution (three teaspoons of soda to one quart water).
- For better cleaning of coffee maker, run it through its cycle with baking soda solution and rinse clean.
- Give baby bottles a good cleaning with soda and hot water.
- Sprinkle soda on barbecue grills, let soak, and then rinse off.
- Polish silverware with dry soda on a damp cloth. Rub, rinse, and dry.
- Reduce odor build-up in dishwasher by sprinkling some baking soda on the bottom.
- Run dishwasher through its cycle with baking soda in it instead of soap to give it a good cleaning.

- To remove burned-on food from a pan, let the pan soak in baking soda and water for ten minutes before washing. Alternately, scrub the pot with dry baking soda and a moist scouring pad.
- For a badly-burned pan with a thick layer of burned-on food, pour a thick layer of baking soda directly onto the bottom of the pan. Then sprinkle on just enough water so as to moisten the soda. Leave the pot overnight. Scrub it clean next day.
- Rub stainless steel and chrome with a moist cloth and dry baking soda to shine it up. Rinse and dry. On stainless steel, scrub in the Directions of the grain.
- Clean plastic, porcelain and glass with dry baking soda on a damp cloth. Rinse and dry.
- Keep drains clean and free-flowing by putting four tablespoons of soda in them each week. Flush the soda down with hot water.
- To remove strong odors from hands, wet hands and rub them hard with baking soda, then rinse.
- Sprinkle baking soda on wet toothbrush and brush teeth and dentures with it.
- Apply soda directly to insect bites, rashes, and poison ivy to relieve discomfort. Make a paste with water.
- For plucking chickens, add one teaspoon of baking soda to the boiling water. The feathers will come off easier and flesh will be clean and white.
- Add to water to soak dried beans to make them more digestible.
- Use to remove melted plastic bread wrapper from toaster, dampen cloth and make a mild abrasive with baking soda.

Lemon juice in the kitchen project

A little lemon juice makes everything taste better. - Virginia Sanborn Burleigh

Lemons originated in India and have been used for trading purposes for centuries. Lemons were originally called "the golden apples." This inexpensive fruit is very useful and versatile.

- To make substitute buttermilk, mix one cup of milk with a tablespoon of lemon juice for a buttermilk substitute that works great!
- To sanitize dishwasher and remove mineral deposits and odors, remove all dishes. Place 1/4 cup of lemon juice in the soap dispenser and run through the normal cycle. Dishwasher will be clean and smell wonderful!
- To clean copper pots, cover the surface of a half lemon with salt and scrub. Rinse and buff with a soft cloth for a beautiful shine.
- To clean silver, clean with lemon juice and buff with a soft cloth.
- Lemon juice also cleans the tarnish off brass.
- To remove the smell of garlic or onions from hands, rub with a lemon slice and rinse.

Salt beyond cooking in the kitchen project

- Salt works very well on ink stains on carpet. If the ink is still wet immediately cover it with salt. Allow the salt to sit overnight then vacuum the area. The salt will absorb the ink. If the ink is already dry wet it thoroughly before trying the salt treatment. Salt works on other stains also, such as drink stains.
- In case of fire in the kitchen pour salt on it. Small fires, on a burner or in the oven, are easily stamped out by pouring a large amount of salt directly on it. In fact, any small household fire can be stamped out by pouring salt on it. Salt is inexpensive making it appealing for other uses.
- Tarnished silver will look practically new again when cleaned with salt. We can also remove mildew with a combination of salt and lemon juice. Mix enough lemon juice in with the salt to make a paste and use it on tubs and shower tiles.

Honey in the kitchen project

Honey is the only food in the world that will not spoil or rot. It will do what some people refer to as "turning to sugar." In reality honey is always honey. However, when left in a cool dark place for a long time it will crystallize.

"You can sweeten two pots with only one drop of honey."
- Deji Badiru, June 22, 2010

"You catch more flies with honey than with vinegar."
– A Common Saying

Both honey and vinegar have their respective uses in the kitchen. For honey's sake, we list the following kitchen uses:

- Tasty additive to foods and drinks
- Use as a sugar substitute when cooking or baking
- **Remedy for diabetic ulcer to speed up the healing process**
- **Relaxant for anxiety and nervousness**
- **Antibacterial solution** — Honey has antibacterial properties due to its acidic nature and produces hydrogen peroxide through an enzymic process
- **Remedy for burns, particularly as first-aid in kitchen accidents**
- **Treatment for sore throat — to grease the passage of food on the gastronomic journey**
- **Enhancement to Vitamin A**
- **Immune system and energy booster**
- **Antiseptic**
- Honey taken with cinnamon powder can ease stomachache
- Good antioxidant

When a honey jar lid hardens, loosen it by boiling some water and placing the honey jar in the hot water. Turn off the heat and let the jar content liquefy. It is then as good as before. Never boil honey or put it in a microwave. To do so will kill the enzymes in the honey.

Facts on Honey and Cinnamon

- It is found that a mixture of honey and Cinnamon cures most diseases.
- Honey is produced in most of the countries of the world.
- Honey can be used without any side effects for any kind of diseases.
- Even though honey is sweet, if taken in the right dosage as a medicine, it does not harm diabetic patients.
- If bladder infection is suspected, take two tablespoons of cinnamon powder and one teaspoon of honey in a glass of lukewarm water and drink it. It can hold off germs temporarily until a consultation can be arranged with a medical practitioner.
- For upset stomach, honey taken with cinnamon powder mitigates stomach ache and also reduces the symptoms of stomach ulcers.
- Some studies suggest that if honey is taken with cinnamon powder, the stomach is relieved of gas.
- It is believed that cinnamon powder sprinkled on two tablespoons of honey, taken before meal, can relieve acidity to facilitate digestion.

Case Example of Diverse Application of Project Management

As with the recommended application in the kitchen, project management is applied in a variety of other areas. The lead author has a personal experience in the application of the concepts of project management in coaching a soccer team. Deji, by default, became the coach of an adult recreational soccer team in Fall 1992 in the Central

Oklahoma Adult Soccer League (COASL). Using project management processes, he took the team from being at the bottom of the league to being the league champion in just three seasons. This was not due to his coaching acumen, but rather, the way he motivated the team and made everyone aware of his respective responsibilities on the team on and off the field.

As a coach-player, the author applied project management techniques to the way he handled team assignments and encouraged the other players to do likewise. He developed a documentation system that, each week, informed the players of where the team stood in relation to other teams. Each week, he handed out written notes about what the current objectives were and how they would be addressed. Because of this, he was nicknamed "Memo Coach." It got to a point where the players got used to being given written assignments, and they would jokingly demand their memo for the week. Copies of graphical representation of the game lineup were given to the players to study prior to each game. Each person had to know his immediate coordination points during a game: who would provide support for whom, who would cover what area of the field, and so on. He applied project management to various aspects of the team including and following:

- Team registration
- Team motivation
- Team communication
- Team cooperation
- Team coordination
- Expected individual commitment
- Player camaraderie
- Field preparation
- Sportsmanship
- Play etiquette
- Game lineup
- Training regimen
- Funding

Everybody had an assignment that was explained and coordinated from the standpoint to total team and game management. In the second season under this unconventional coach, the team took third place. The players were all excited and motivated and credited the success to the way the management of the team was handled. So, starting the third season, everyone came out highly charged up to move the team forward to an even better season. Of course, there was the season's inaugural memo waiting for the team.

One of the favorite memos handed out to the team was the one that indicated the team's track record (Win-Lose-Draw) dating back 10 years. With this, the coach was able to motivate the team that it was time to move to the higher levels of the league. Traditionally, the team has been viewed as one of the "so-so" teams in the league. Not a bad team, but not among the best either. The coach convinced the players that while winning was not everything (particularly in an adult soccer league), it sure would feel better than losing. This was in an "over-30" league, tactfully referred to as the masters league, where most of the players were technical or business professionals.

With the high level of motivation, division of labor, and effective utilization of existing resources (soccer skills, or lack thereof), the team was crowned the league champion for Fall 1993. This is not a small feat in a league that contained traditional powerhouses. It is interesting to note that the achievement was made with little or no recruitment of additional "skillful" players, who were in short supply anyway in that league at that time. This shows that with proper management, existing resources of a team can be leveraged to achieve an unprecedented level of improvement both in direct skills development as well as total team and game management. In particular, using the techniques of project management for soccer management has many advantages including the following:

- Better connection with other players
- More traceable lines of communication
- More sustainable levels of cooperation

- Better pathways of coordination
- Holistic systems view of soccer game scenarios

With this case example, we believe a case for project management in the kitchen has been made. Have a great kitchen project!

APPENDIX

Conversion Factors for Kitchen Project Management

Kitchen Measurements

A pinch 1/8 ……….....…less than teaspoon
3 teaspoons (tsp) …………1 tablespoon (tbsp)
2 tablespoons…………………………....………1/8 cup
4 tablespoons…………………………………………1/4 cup
16 tablespoons…………………………………………..1cup
5 tbsp. + 1 tsp……………………………………1/3 cup
4 ounces (oz)…………………....……………………1/2 cup
8 ounces (oz)……………………....…………………1 cup
16 ounces (oz)……....…2 cups…………(453 grams) 1 pound (lb)
1 ounce………………………………………....………..2 tbsp
1 cup of liquid…………………………………1/2 pint
2 cups…………………………………………………1 pint
2 pint……………………………………………1 quart
4 cups of liquid…………....………………..1 quart
4 quarts…………....………………………1gallon
8 quarts……………....…1 peck (apples, pears, etc.)
1 jigger………………1-1/2 fl ounces (fl oz)
1 jigger…………………3 tablespoons

Scientific Notation of Numbers

Notation	Expansion
yotta (10^{24}):	1, 000, 000, 000, 000, 000, 000, 000, 000
zetta (10^{21}):	1, 000, 000, 000, 00,0 000, 000, 000
exa (10^{18}):	1, 000, 000, 000, 000, 000, 000
peta (10^{15}):	1, 000, 000, 000, 000, 000
tera (10^{12}):	1, 000, 000, 000, 000
giga (10^{9}):	1, 000, 000, 000
mega (10^{6}):	1, 000, 000
kilo (10^{3}):	1, 000
hecto (10^{2}):	100
deca (10^{1}):	10
deci (10^{-1}):	0.1
centi (10^{-2}):	0.01
milli (10^{-3}):	0.001
micro (10^{-6}):	0.000 001
nano (10^{-9}):	0.000 000 001
pico (10^{-12}):	0.000 000 000 001
femto (10^{-15}):	0.000 000 000 000 001
atto (10^{-18}):	0.000 000 000 000 000 001
zepto (10^{-21}):	0.000 000 000 000 000 000 001
yocto (10^{-24}):	0.000 000 000 000 000 000 000 001
stringo (10^{-35}):	0.000 000 000 000 000 000 000 000 000 000 000 01

Area Conversion

English system

1 foot (ft)	= 12 inches (in) 1'=12"	in
1 yard (yd)	= 3 feet	ft
1 mile (mi)	= 1760 yards	yd
1 sq. foot	= 144 sq. inches	sq in
1 sq. yard	= 9 sq. feet	sq ft
1 acre	= 4840 sq. yards = 43560 ft^2	sq yd
1 sq. mile	= 640 acres	acres

Metric numbers

mm	millimeter	.001 m
cm	centimeter	.01 m
dm	decimeter	.1 m
m	meter	1 m
dam	decameter	10 m
hm	hectometer	100 m
km	kilometer	1000 m

Multiply	By	To Obtain
acres	43,560	sq feet
	4,047	sq meters
	4,840	sq yards
	0.405	hectare
sq cm	0.155	sq inches
sq feet	144	sq inches
	0.09290	sq meters
	0.1111	sq yards
sq inches	645.16	sq millimeters
sq kilometers	0.3861	sq miles
sq meters	10.764	sq feet
	1.196	sq yards
sq miles	640	acres
	2.590	sq kilometers

144 square inches = 1 square foot
9 square feet = 1 square yard
43,560 square feet = 1 acre
640 acres = 1 square mile
30-1/4 square yards = 1 square rod
40 square rods = 1 square rood
4 square roods = 1 acre
272-1/4 square feet = 1 square rod

Distance Conversion

Multiply	by	to obtain
angstrom	10^{-10}	meters
feet	0.30480	meters
	12	inches
inches	25.40	millimeters
	0.02540	meters
	0.08333	feet
kilometers	3280.8	feet
	0.6214	miles
	1094	yards
meters	39.370	inches
	3.2808	feet
	1.094	yards
miles	5280	feet
	1.6093	kilometers
	0.8694	nautical miles
millimeters	0.03937	inches

nautical miles	6076	feet
	1.852	kilometers
yards	0.9144	meters
	3	feet
	36	inches

Speed Conversion

Multiply	by	to obtain
feet/minute	5.080	mm/second
feet/second	0.3048	meters/second
inches/second	0.0254	meters/second
km/hour	0.6214	miles/hour
meters/second	3.2808	feet/second
	2.237	miles/hour
miles/hour	88.0	feet/minute
	0.44704	meters/second
	1.6093	km/hour
	0.8684	knots
knot	1.151	miles/hour

Weight Conversion

Multiply	by	to obtain
carat	0.200	cubic grams
grams	0.03527	ounces
kilograms	2.2046	pounds
ounces	28.350	grams
pound	16	ounces
	453.6	grams
stone (UK)	6.35	kilograms
	14	pounds
ton (net)	907.2	kilograms

	2000	pounds
	0.893	gross tons
	0.907	metric tons
ton (gross)	2240	pounds
	1.12	net tons
	1.016	metric tons
tonne (metric)	2,204.623	pounds
	0.984	gross pound
	1000	kilograms

Volume Conversion

Multiply	by	to obtain
acre-foot	1233.5	cubic meters
cubic cm	0.06102	cubic inches
cubic feet	1728	cubic inches
	7.480	gallons (US)
	0.02832	cubic meters
	0.03704	cubic yards
liter	1.057	liquid quarts
	0.908	dry quarts
	61.024	cubic inches
gallons (US)	231	cubic inches
	3.7854	liters
	4	quarts
	0.833	British gallons
	128	U.S. fluid ounces
quarts (US)	0.9463	liters

Power Conversion

Multiply	by	to obtain
BTU	1055.9	joules
	0.2520	kg-calories
watt-hour	3600	joules
	3.409	BTU
HP (electric)	746	watts
BTU/second	1055.9	watts
watt-second	1.00	joules

Temperature Conversion

Celsius to Kelvin	$K = C + 273.15$
Celsius to Fahrenheit	$F = (9/5)C + 32$
Fahrenheit to Celsius	$C = (5/9)(F - 32)$
Fahrenheit to Kelvin	$K = (5/9)(F + 459.67)$
Fahrenheit to Rankin	$R = F + 459.67$
Rankin to Kelvin	$K = (5/9)R$

Pressure Conversion

Multiply	by	to obtain
atmospheres	1.01325	bars
	33.90	feet of water
	29.92	inches of mercury
	760.0	mm of mercury
bar	75.01	cm of mercury
	14.50	pounds/sq inch
dyne/sq cm	0.1	N/sq meter

newtons/sq cm	1.450	pounds/sq inch
pounds/sq inch	0.06805	atmospheres
	2.036	inches of mercury
	27.708	inches of water
	68.948	millibars
	51.72	mm of mercury

Velocity Conversion

Speed of light	$2.997,925 \times 10^{10}$ cm/sec
	983.6×10^{10} ft/sec
	186,284 miles/sec
Velocity of sound	340.3 meters/sec
	1116 ft/sec
	1116 ft/sec
Gravity (acceleration)	9.80665 m/sec square
	32.174 ft/sec square
	386.089 inches/sec square

12 inches	=	1 foot	
3 feet	=	1 yard	
5-1/2 yards	=	1 rod	
6 feet	=	1 fathom	
40 rods	=	1 furlong	
8 furlongs	=	1 mile	
1760 yards	=	1 mile	
5280 feet	=	1 mile	
60 sea miles	=	1 degree	
0.8684 miles	=	1 sea mile1 radian	$= 57.3°$
1 inch	=	2.54 cm	
1 gallon	=	231 in^3	
1 kilogram	=	2.205 lb	

1 newton	=	$1 \text{ kg} \bullet \text{m/s}^2$
1 joule	=	$1 \text{ N} \bullet \text{m}$
1 watt	=	1 J/s
1 pascal	=	1 N/m^2
1 BTU	=	778 ft-lb
	=	252 cal
	=	1,054.8 J
1 horsepower	=	745.7 W
1 atmosphere	=	14.7 lb/in^2
	=	$1.01 \bullet 10^5 \text{ N/m}^2$

Measures Conversion

Liquid Measure	Dry Measure
4 gills = 1 pint	2 pints = 1 quart
2 pints = 1 quart	8 quarts = 1 peck
4 quart = 1 gallon	4 pecks = 1 bushel
31-1/2 gallons = 1 barrel	36 bushels = 1 chaldron
231 cu. In. = 1 gallon	2,150.42 cu. In. = 1 standard bushel
	1 cubic foot = approx. 4/5 bushel

Printed in the United States
By Bookmasters